Breaking Up & Divorce 5 Steps: How To Heal and Be Comfortable Alone

Breaking Up & Divorce 5 Steps: How To Heal and Be Comfortable Alone

THE RELATIONSHIP FORMULA WORKBOOK SERIES

Jill P. Weber, Ph.D.

ISBN: 1533000972
ISBN 13: 9781533000972
Library of Congress Control Number: 2016907357
CreateSpace Independent Publishing Platform
North Charleston, South Carolina

About the Author

Jill P. Weber, PhD, is a clinical psychologist in private practice in Washington, DC. She is the author of *Having Sex, Wanting Intimacy: Why Women Settle for One-Sided Relationships*. She writes a relationship and self-esteem blog for *Psychology Today*. Her writing has appeared in *Huffington Post*, *Healthy Living Magazine*, and *USA Today*, and she is a psychology contributor to various media outlets, including the *Washington Post*, *Nightline*, CNN, Discovery Channel, and the Associated Press.

The Relationship Formula Workbook Series

Contents

Preface

People experience many types of loss yet frequently avoid or minimize their distress. Whether the loss is childhood trauma, death of a loved one, or the end of a crush of a few months, a two-year serious relationship, or a long-term marriage, it's always okay to allow yourself to acknowledge your sadness about having missed out on something or about losing something very dear. Perhaps your loss occurred yesterday when the object of your affection stopped returning your texts and ignored your phone calls, or maybe you're going through a divorce to a long-term partner and father or mother of your children. The human brain's unhealthy ability to stifle feelings about loss may lead you to tell yourself to "just keep moving," as if perpetual activity and motion will somehow take away the heart's ache.

If you struggle with chronic relationship issues, or feel as if you can't seem to get your needs met in romantic relationships, or believe you can't find a "real" relationship, chances are you need to come to terms with your past. Loss is tricky because each time you have a new one, it triggers memories of earlier disappointments, and the accumulation of negative feelings may overwhelm.

You may avoid accepting your loss because you are afraid that you can't handle the difficult feelings that acceptance will evoke or that it will render you weak. In some cases, people fear that acknowledging a rejection may bring such insecurity that they will be unable to function. Avoiding grief may seem to you like healthy coping—that you are just trying to keep up with life. Unfortunately, the reality looks somewhat different.

When you don't allow yourself to acknowledge the feelings that your losses evoke, you walk around with unprocessed emotion running through your mind. This negative energy influences future choices in a potentially damaging way. It's akin to living your life with a perpetual itch at the center of your back that you just can't reach. You try to ignore it, but you often find it's distracting you from the task at hand and blocking you from being fully in the present. This residual itch chronically irritates, but you tell yourself it's not there, that it's "all in your head"—yet its presence intrudes.

Many will seek distraction from loss in new and hastily established relationships where they may temporarily ride a high. Believing that finding a mate is the only way to relieve the discomfort, they embark on a frantic mission to couple up. Others hold on to unhappy, dulled-out relationships out of fear of being left on their own and not being able to move on from the loss. And yet, others avoid confronting the loss through keeping the memory of old romantic partners, who have long since moved on, alive in their minds by obsessing about the demise of their relationships or endlessly wondering what their partners are thinking, or mentally replaying angry fights, disappointments, or good times in the relationships.

If you are doing any of this, it means the residual itch has too much influence in your life, and this makes you vulnerable. The only way to lose it is by accepting and working through your loss. Learning how to end unfulfilling relationships or how to accept their end and to healthfully be alone, will tremendously improve the likelihood of securing a better match in the future. The exercises that follow are designed to help you do just that.

Mutually reciprocated love is not always possible, and recognizing when it's not and allowing it to end can be a meaningfully positive aspect of the human experience. It is inevitable if you are living and loving that, at some point, you will get hurt. After all, what would life be like if you never skinned your knee—would you truly be alive? Even when things haven't gone the way you wish with love and romance, you may still celebrate your ability and willingness to love and let others into your heart. Just like a fire that burns a forest, making way for new life, the despair and heartache will, if you allow it, give way to new personal growth. The potent feelings of exhilaration that come with finding love and connection will come again. But for now, you need to acknowledge what you no longer have.

Were all stars to disappear or die,
I should learn to look at an empty sky
And feel its total dark sublime,
Though this might take me a little time.
"The More Loving One," by Auden

Special note: Keep a notebook handy so you can write down your answers to the exercises in this workbook. Review the notebook from time to time to remind yourself of what you are learning about yourself as you grow through this program. The more you review the material, the more the tools you've been practicing will become automatic.

STEP 1

Accept You Need to Let Go

Some tell themselves, "No, this step isn't for me. It's not that big of a deal; I wouldn't call it grief," or "I'm not sure my loss qualifies." Even if the loss seems small to you, give yourself permission to take it seriously. Grief does not require a justification. If you had someone you cared about in your life and now he or she is gone or no longer available to you in the same way, you need to recognize this as a significant loss.

If you're experiencing romantic heartbreak or struggling to end something you know is not good for you, keep in mind that earlier, unprocessed emotional losses will amplify current upsets. For example, as a child, were you denied something you should deserve by right of being a human being—respectful, loving treatment by your parents, adequate health care, nutrition, basic financial resources? Childhood losses can intensify adult romantic loss.

Acceptance does not mean you like it, but it does mean that you stop beating your head against the wall and spinning your wheels trying to get something that is never going to come. The way to soothe this upset is to remind yourself that there are other ways to get what you want.

Generally people hold on to unhappy unions or obsess about an ex in order to avoid the pain of letting go.

Problem: You're not sure you *want to* end your romantic relationship or *accept* its ending.
Cure: Heed the red flags.

Are you obsessing about a romantic interest? Are you leaving text messages or doing drive-bys hoping to spot the object of your desire? Are you in a frenzy to see him or her, working to connect, wanting to spend time with him or her despite lack of interest or dismissiveness?

The project of turning an aloof partner into someone who is warm and connected to you typically never delivers. The one in pursuit is left to feel even more rejected and insecure about his or her very nature.

The urge to correct a wrong or recalibrate a relationship is natural and oftentimes healthy. This urge can become dysfunctional when it's channeled into an obsessive and frenetic attempt to make a romantic relationship more than it can actually be.

Exercise: Identify Red Flags

You may feel all you want is to keep or to create a relationship with a particular person. And perhaps, you have put him or her on a bit of a pedestal. Some tell themselves that the object of their affection is perfect or that what they once had was perfect; the fact is, it wasn't really perfect if it's over or if you are not getting what you need. Right? Take off the rose-colored glasses and put on the prescription lenses. Take a hard, cold look at who your ex (or emotionally unavailable love interest) really is. What is his or her emotional capacity for intimacy? What is his or her track record with love?

Universal red flags that need be considered and taken seriously:

- If your partner or love interest makes plans with you and then backs out, cancels, and makes excuses as to why he or she did not deliver, deeply consider that this person may not be able to provide a healthy, emotionally reciprocal relationship. Plans change occasionally, but he or she should respectfully let you know. Notice if you are spending excessive time waiting around, hoping and wondering if he or she will contact you.

- Believe the behavior your romantic partner is displaying (i.e., is the person passive-aggressive, avoidant, or often noncommittal in his or her attitude with you?). It is common when attracted to someone to want to rationalize his or her poor behavior. If someone treats you with disrespect or chronically lets you down, take this as data that reveals to you who this person actually is. If he or she dismisses you or justifies mistreatment of you, take this seriously; it means this person may not be a suitable match.

- If a potential romantic interest is not looking for "anything serious" or needs a lot of "space," stop approaching and let them go. This means he or she is not in the same place you are and may not want the same things you want.

- Believe what your romantic interest or partner is verbally communicating about himself or herself. If a romantic interest regularly (more than once in a while) communicates in a way that leaves you feeling hurt, talk with him or her about it. If he or she can't hear you or take your feelings seriously, move on. Instead of overworking the relationship and trying to right the wrong, accept that the match is not viable. It is not your job to bring your partners along or to show them a better way. It is your job to work on growing as a person.

- Does it feel as if you see your partner more on his or her terms than on your own? If so, pull back. You are overfunctioning, and your partner is underdelivering.

A relationship cannot run on fumes alone. Feeling low energy from your partner and having a sense that you are doing all of the work are red flags. Consider that you may need to let this one go.

Self-Assessment: Observe the Red Flags in Your Current or Past Relationship

- Write down red flags that you have noticed flying overhead. Were they red flags you noticed early on or later in the relationship? Use examples from above or write your own.

- Are you rationalizing your partner's disappointing behavior? Maybe telling yourself that it's your fault or that if you do something differently, perhaps he or she will change? Remember, it's impossible to build up a relationship if you are the only one doing the work. Write down rationalizations for these red flags that you use to justify your continuing efforts.

- Are you neglecting yourself by focusing all of your attention on sustaining the unsustainable?

Problem: "Although I'm unhappy, I keep telling myself that the situation will get better and work itself out or that I just need to try harder."
Cure: Develop awareness for your dysfunctional relationship pattern.

So often, people feel very unhappy in long-term relationships but tell themselves that it will get better and to "hang in there" a bit longer. The reasons for this vary: some feel guilty throwing in the towel, others feel it would be an admission of failure to let go of a marriage or long-term commitment, and still others feel afraid of being alone and don't know a path out of codependence.

Exercise: Identify Your Relationship Pattern

Here are a few relationship dynamics that are entirely dysfunctional and that people put up with in the hopes that things will get better. Eventually (sometimes after twenty years), something breaks, and it may finally end. These people tell me they wish they would have done it sooner, and they struggle to understand why they kept investing more and more of their energy, time, and emotional resources into someone who was making them perpetually unhappy. Do you see yourself in any of these situations? Or is there a scenario that better describes your relationship dynamic?

- **The Avoider:** Ana felt perpetually dismissed by her boyfriend, Pete. Every time she sought to discuss their weekend plans, their future goals, or when they would see each other next, he pushed her away with a sour mood. If talking about the practicalities of life were hard, Pete certainly wouldn't hear her emotional ups and downs or deepest yearnings. Eventually, Ana would become so fed up with feeling dismissed that she would stop reaching out. Just as Ana would let go and not try so hard, Pete would suddenly fall into a good mood. They would have a warm talk or a fun afternoon together. She subsisted on these small morsels of intimacy when, by and large, most of the rest of her time with him was lonely.

- **The Addict:** John fell madly and deeply in love with Sara. He knew she was the one for him. After they had difficulty conceiving, she began to drink more and more alcohol. When he tried to talk to her about it, she would deny that alcohol was an issue for her. He lived his life trying to anticipate Sara's life and needs at the expense of himself. Sara went through periods of depressions and irritability, and John always felt responsible— like it was his job to make her feel better. Occasionally, he would suggest that she needed help that he couldn't give her, but the moment she became defensive, he would give this up and go back to the work of making sure she was okay—to no avail.

- **The Narcissist:** For Clint, everything was about his partner, Josh. He wanted Josh to be happy, and that made him happy. Early on in their courtship, this felt good to Clint but after a few years in, he started to feel used and as if there was no role for him outside of what he did for Josh. Josh was the primary breadwinner, and this contributed to Clint's belief that he had no leverage. He could only do what Josh wanted. When he complained about this dynamic, Josh would make a joke and go back to business as usual. Clint felt compelled to live his life on Josh's terms, go to restaurants that Josh wanted, hang out with Josh's friends, go on trips ınted, spend money the way Josh wanted. Over time, Clint ͺrget who he was and what he liked or disliked. He felt as if he ͺy an extension of Josh.

- ͺ **ͺotional Cripple:** Mimi worked for eighteen years to make sure her partner, Samantha, was emotionally stable. When they first met, Mimi felt compassion for some difficulties Samantha had while growing up. After a few years of being together, Mimi realized Samantha had an extensive trauma history. Samantha was plagued by her childhood and as a result, lived in a kind of dysfunctional state—she had difficulty working, interacting with their children, paying bills, dealing with the maintenance of the home, keeping up social connections. Mimi continued to have empathy for Samantha and so did all of these things to her full capacity. She worked hard so as to not add extra burden to Samantha's life. Samantha never took responsibility for her mental health through seeing a therapist. Mimi accepted this by compulsively working to pick up the slack.

- **Two Ships Passing In the Night:** Sasha and Simon always operated well together. From the beginning of their courtship, they let each other do their own thing and then met in the middle when it worked for both of them. Over time, with children and jobs, the meeting in the middle happened less and less. Eventually, they existed as two separate entities living in the same house—they interacted over household tasks and childcare but otherwise did not share the intimate details of their lives or feelings. When they would have to go out to dinner or be alone, they struggled to feel comfortable and at ease. They constantly sought distractions to avoid emotionally intimate interaction.

Do you see yourself and your partner in any of these stories? If the answer is "yes," talk with your partner about entering couples therapy. If he or she is unwilling, consider if you alone can sustain this union and also be happy and healthy within yourself.

He wouldn't do it

Problem: "Divorce scares me."
Cure: Educate yourself with the facts.

As a psychologist, I often meet with couples and individuals who come to me to work more intensely and systematically on their relationships. For many, this is a healthy desire that their partners reciprocate, and together they begin the journey to a healthier, happier union. Others, however, find themselves stuck—unable to improve the relationship and unable to leave it. These folks usually don't want to leave because they fear, understandably, the uncertainty of change and of being alone.

For married couples and life partners, it's a good idea to keep working on the marriage/partnership when both are invested and committed. Otherwise, if you find yourself stuck in the same old disappointing patterns, you may wish to tackle the fear you harbor about being alone, uncoupled, or being a divorced person. It's important to not allow fear or a sense of shame to make your decisions for you. Recognize that, in some cases, ending a long-term, committed relationship is the right decision.

Consider What Positives Divorce May Bring to Your Life

- **It is not always better for the kids to stay married:** It is heart wrenching for many who are chronically unhappy in a marriage to even consider the idea of divorce because of fear that it will forever harm their children. It's essential to take children's feelings about divorce seriously and to empathize and help them to talk about how it impacts them (*not you*). However, the notion that staying in a bad marriage is somehow better for kids is dubious. What is more harmful and even traumatizing to children is spending a great deal of time in a home filled with negative emotion, perpetual sadness, tension, or chronic conflict. Children tend to absorb these feelings and may believe they are responsible for them in some way. If you are in a chronically unhappy union and eventually make a thoughtful decision to end it, you are modeling for your children that they do not have to be passive participants in their own unhappiness.

- **You'll improve your physical health and emotional well-being:** Healthy couples are able to resolve disagreements in a way that makes both feel better about the issue at hand. A couple may even feel closer as a result of the disagreement. However, when negative relationship dynamics chronically play out between partners, resentment grows. Before you know it, not picking up milk on the way home becomes a knockdown, drag-out fight. When there is no resolution to chronic marital distress, both partners live in a fight-or-flight state. They may have difficulty sleeping or eating healthfully or trouble with short-term memory; they may gain weight and fail to go to the doctor or nurture themselves emotionally. Their cup is so full, between work, children, and the chronic negative emotion, that there is no room for self-care. The toll negative relationships take on physical health should not be underestimated. There is research to suggest that chronically negative or abusive relationships can shorten one's lifespan. Ending a toxic union is the first step in a chain of events that leads to taking better care of one's self.

- **You'll open the door to find a more fulfilling love:** Sometimes, working through a difficult marriage and developing greater self-awareness around what your role may have been in its demise can open the door to a path that leads to a happier union. If after thoughtful work on yourself and your own weaknesses and consideration of your partner, you do not notice progress in your marriage, then the longer you stay, the longer you deny yourself the right to romantic happiness. Don't fear facing the world alone; fear spending a lifetime with someone with whom you are unhappy. Fear of being alone is not an adequate reason to stay in a marriage and actually increases the misery, as one comes to feel trapped and powerless.

- **The grief will pass:** As hard as ending a relationship can be, many find that they learn something valuable from the heartache. For example, they become more connected with family and friends, they pull more meaning from the relationships they do have, they connect with feelings of gratitude, or they have an easier time not sweating the small stuff. The problem comes *not* for those who experience grief, which is a natural and essential step in processing divorce, but for those who do not allow themselves to take the time necessary to grieve and adjust.

- **It is liberating to give up the fantasy that things will improve:** If you are in a committed relationship that is filled with discontent for prolonged periods of time, you probably try to tell yourself, "Things will get better." Although in the moment, this thought can be relieving, in the long run, it sets people up for defeat and disappointment when things don't actually get better. If you and your partner are not taking active steps to improve the relationship, are not noticing small improvements, and are not both equally committed to this work, then simply hoping things will get better could keep you stuck in a no-win situation.

Confront your fear of divorce. For most people, the pain of leaving eventually passes. Breaking up is *not* the worst thing ever.

Exercise: Rethink Divorce Stigma

Now, generate some of your own greatest fears about divorce or permanent separation from a long-term partner. Write your most upsetting fear or catastrophic thought, and then next to it write the good that could come from that same fear. Search for the silver lining—you're not denying the pain the loss brings but are looking for what positives could also come from letting go.

Example:
Negative consequence: The children will not grow up with both parents in the home.
Positive consequence: The children will be exposed to less fighting and negative emotion or less exposed to an unloving model of what marriage "should" be.

Negative consequence: I will be completely alone in the world.
Positive consequence: I will have the space to build a fuller life that reflects my real self.

Negative consequence:
Positive consequence:

Negative consequence:
Positive consequence:

Negative consequence:
Positive consequence:

Negative consequence:
Positive consequence:

Negative consequence:
Positive consequence:

Problem: "I can't find the courage, motivation, or determination to face my pain, work through my loss, and start over."
Cure: Remember a time when you struggled and came out on top.

Margie had the rug pulled out from under her when the love of her life stood in the doorway with bag packed and announced he was leaving her. She was devastated. She was so depleted she couldn't even imagine getting up for work, taking out the trash, or cooking a meal. After a month of this, she remembered a very hard experience she'd had as a teenager when she felt all of her friends turn against her. Defeated and alone, she started talking to different kinds of people and became more open to new experiences and new types. A year later, she had meaningful friendships and was doing well in school. She marveled at how reaching out and trying made so much of a difference and told herself she could do that again.

For Matt, after his partner left him, he felt panic and fear for the future. Then he remembered coming out as a gay man and the terror this induced and how eventually that terror led to freedom and greater acceptance of himself. Keeping this in mind eased his fear of being alone and, with time, he came to believe that whatever happened, he would be okay.

Jamie worked hard to hide from herself what deep down she knew all along— her marriage was not making her happy. Nevertheless, she did not have the confidence to break away for a new start. Then she remembered when she was a young adult, living alone and enjoying it, feeling empowered that she had her own space and was calling the shots in her life.

Exercise: Build Resiliency

Remember another point in your life when you got through something difficult and rebounded. Examples include losing a close friend or boyfriend/girlfriend, moving and then having to create a whole new life, coming to terms with a medical or psychiatric diagnosis, facing your parents' divorce, managing a learning disability, tolerating being bullied.

Self-Assessment: How Have You Already Been Resilient?

- Think back on your *childhood* and *teenage* years. Can you remember a time when things were difficult? Some people recall these events easily and for others, it is more difficult. Everyone has had periods of special difficulty. If at first you can't find one, keep thinking. In your notebook, write down as many scenarios as you can recall.
- How did the situation resolve? Did you do something differently? Did time heal it, did luck heal it, or did someone else intervene on your behalf? Write down how eventually the situation(s) went away, improved, or no longer became a focus of your attention.
- What would you do differently if you were in this situation again today? What would you tell yourself about it in hindsight?
- Now, think back on your *adult* self—twenties, thirties, or forties. Recall a situation or situations when things were difficult for you—starting at your college, moving to a new city, finding a job, having a baby, getting a degree, or experiencing financial hardships or a traumatic family or personal event.
- How did the situation resolve? Did you do something differently? Did time heal it, did luck fix it, or did someone else intervene on your behalf? Write down how eventually the situation ended.

- What would you do differently if you were in this situation again today? What would you tell yourself about it in retrospect?
- You likely have a perspective now that you didn't have then. Try to imagine that one day you will feel similarly about what you are experiencing at this moment. See if the voice in your head (the one telling you how awful all of this is, that you can't cope, that you're a failure, or that your life is over) can give you perspective by saying something that you wish someone would have told you at the time of your previous hardship(s)—"This will get better," "It seems awful now but it won't always be," "You are a strong and capable person," "You will grow from this," "This is not a failure," "You are not a failure," "This is not the end." Write down this new perspective in your notebook, even if you are not entirely sure you believe it yet.

STEP 2

How to Let Go

Kate was just finishing putting her two young sons to bed; kissing them good-night and reading bedtime stories were her favorite parts of the day. When she closed her younger son's bedroom door, her husband's presence took her by surprise. She didn't expect him to be home for another few hours as he typically worked late at his law practice. Forlorn, he looked seriously in her eyes. After a few minutes, he said, "I can't do this anymore. I'm sorry."

Kate couldn't believe what she was hearing. Shocked, she responded, "What do you mean…you don't mean us? You can't do us anymore?"

Looking down at his shoes, all he could muster was, "I'm sorry."

Adrenaline pumped through every vein in her body, a thousand questions flooded her brain, and she felt her knees go weak. In Kate's mind, all she had been doing for the past fifteen years was working to keep their family intact. She managed bouts of loneliness by telling herself that her husband was working long days for her happiness and for their children's futures. She was his cheerleader when he struggled with his mood and his work. She took pride in being the rock, *his rock*, and now he was leaving *her*? Physically struggling, emotionally shocked, she mumbled, "Is there someone else?"

After a long pause, he responded: "Yes, I am in love with her." And that was it. He walked out the front door. Fifteen years of marriage gone in a few moments of time.

When we are suddenly confronted with a great loss, our bodies and minds reel. Hearts racing, veins on fire, people have trouble thinking clearly. People grow physically weak and agitated at the same time. They oscillate between emotional numbness and emotional chaos. All of this makes them believe they are going crazy, but they are not—you are not—this is normal.

Waves of upsetting emotions—anger, confusion, sadness, anxiety, panic—flood the system. This flood of emotion hijacks rational thought, making it very difficult to get a handle on what just happened and how to begin recovery. It can be relieving to remind yourself that *grief is a well-documented five-stage process.*

As you come to terms with the end of a relationship, you will likely go in and out of these stages, and it helps to know where you are in this process. Also, this is a good time to consider your history with loss. Sometimes, people hold on to relationships to avoid having to experience previous losses and unprocessed grief from the past. This is an opportunity to deal with this past. Learn how to shake hands with your losses; invite them in so you don't have to avoid and live in fear of them any longer.

Stages of Grief

There are five stages to grief. Elizabeth Kubler-Ross originally identified and described these stages in her groundbreaking book *On Death and Dying,* published in 1969. When people mourn a loss—including not just a death but a breakup, a divorce, or the loss of a relationship, a job, or a pet—all people, regardless of culture or ethnicity, tend to pass through specific stages in processing the loss. Most important for you to know is that passing through these stages is considered normal and healthy grieving.

The stages are not fixed but are fluid. They do not necessarily occur in a specific order, so sometimes people go back and forth between the stages. It's normal to feel better at times and then find yourself back in a place of shock or anger or despair—this is how the grieving process works. Eventually, the resolution is calm acceptance.

There is no timetable or "right" way to pass through the stages of loss. Taking note of where you are in this process from time to time will help you to feel grounded and normal. The stages of grief are described below in the context of the loss of a relationship rather than the death of a loved one.

1. **Denial:** The fear, the terror, the can't-eat-can't sleep-fight-or-flight response can be so overwhelming that more than a few opt out by going into denial. The hallmark of this stage is *difficulty accepting the new reality of your relationship.* If you are in this stage, you may be making frantic efforts to contact your ex or have a strong desire to gain his or her attention. You want to talk, rehash, and ask your ex to see the light or to better understand your perspective. You are looking for ways out of the situation at hand and have a strong sense that "this can't be happening," and "we can still make this work."

2. **Anger:** As denial wanes, anger begins to take its place—"How can this happen to me?," or "After all I have been through, this isn't fair," or "Why does God hate me?," and "I don't deserve this!" For many, this devolves into blaming the ex: "How could she do this to me?" or "After all I have done for her!" Anger can also get turned inward, through self-critical thinking and self-blame: "This is what I deserve," and "I ruin everything."

3. **Bargaining:** This is a feeling of wanting to undo the cause of the grief. "Maybe if I do this or that differently, he won't leave," or "Maybe I can reform my ways and get her back." It may mean seeking the ex out and trying to convince him or her that you have changed and can do better, or guilting them into getting back together with you, or trying to give the ex something to sweeten the pot (i.e., open relationships, less nagging).

4. **Depression:** When bargaining fails, life becomes empty. You know you're in this stage when you feel sad and alone and experience a lack of hope that things will ever get better or that new love will come into your life. At this stage, you may turn introspective, withdraw, and feel a lack of interest in your usual activities. People in this stage sometimes think—"What's the point of trying anymore?" or "Nothing ever works out for me."

5. **Acceptance:** Sadness eventually gives way to acceptance. You will know you're experiencing this stage when you spend less time obsessing about

the loss. You also stop wrangling to become what you think your ex might want. A bonus at this point for some people is the materialization of a new sense of purpose and meaning. They become engaged in new activities or reengage old pursuits. In this stage, you start to believe that you still can have a good life even with the experience of the loss. There is hope, a sense of resilience that you can persevere in spite of everything. Many experience an internal sense of hardiness from having gone through the loss and successfully coming out on the other side—this brings calmness and gratitude.

Whether you or your partner initiated the ending of your relationship, you still have to go through these stages. For some, this process begins before a person officially leaves the relationship.

Instead of experiencing a sense of ongoing despair and fear that the emotional pain will never end, give yourself over to the *process of letting go*. Recognizing what you are experiencing when you are experiencing it makes letting go a doable activity with an eventual end date.

As you embark on this process, note where you are in these stages. Going back and forth is a natural part of grief work. Do not criticize yourself for staying in a particular stage longer than you wish or for skipping a stage altogether. Know that the pain you are experiencing will eventually ease; this is a universal truth.

Problem: "I feel humiliated, embarrassed, and/or a desire to isolate."
Cure: Tell people.

The conflict and fighting that precedes a relationship ending can go on for some time before the relationship is actually over. The turmoil is often so embarrassing to the people in the relationship that they may hide how unhappy they are from their families or close friends. For some, by the time the relationship ends, they feel isolated and as if they do not have anyone to turn to. A sense of shame and a desire to isolate can be toxic to recovery.

The more you share with others what you have been going through, the more connected you will feel to the world around you.

Express your feelings to trusted others—through writing, going to support groups or therapy, emailing/texting old friends, visiting your family—however you wish. Just make sure you find ways to talk about your experience. As you express your feelings, the loss will become more real, and you will have greater awareness for what happened in the relationship and of what you are feeling emotionally.

One person put it to me this way: "After he broke up with me, I stayed on my best friend's couch for three days. I followed her around everywhere she went and just kept repeating the same things that upset me about the breakup and the relationship. I even followed her to do her laundry and take out the trash. But after the third day, I stopped constantly obsessing about him, and I felt better because I knew she understood me, and that helped me understand myself."

Force yourself to talk—let trusted others know about your struggle and pain. If you do not have a close friend or family member, join a support group. Most will be glad you shared with them, and it will help them to feel closer to you. Some will listen attentively and be able to validate your feelings or even talk about their own past heartbreaks or divorce, reminding you that it will get better. Others, however, may invalidate you through telling you: "Get over it!," or "Stop thinking about him," or "You've got to get on with your life." These kinds of sentiments are not particularly helpful, but don't let them stop you from expressing what you are going through. Part of healing is sharing. Even if people don't have a helpful reaction, it's still to your benefit to talk about it. If people invalidate you, dismiss you, or trivialize your feelings, keep in mind that attitude says more about them than about you. You are on the path to recovery, and part of that path is to be authentic with others about the pain and loss you're experiencing.

Special note about divorce: If you are going through a divorce, it can be extremely helpful to talk with an attorney. Initially ask for information about what the divorce process looks like in your state and what you need to get in order for financial and child custody arrangements. The more you arm yourself with the facts, the less panic and fear you will experience about this life change.

Problem: You can't calm down; you feel agitated, restless, uncomfortable in your own skin.
Cure: Intentionally create your own tranquility.

One of the most brutal parts about letting someone go is the heart-racing, adrenaline-pumping physical experience. When going through the shock of losing a close other, you may find that you can't sleep or that you wake in the middle of the night in a panic. You may walk around your home, restless but aimless, uncomfortable but with no sense of how to regain peace. You are "love sick." It will get better, but relief is not instant. It can be helpful during this time to search for moments of peace and for ways to let go of repetitive negative thoughts. It's okay for bits of time to forget about the crisis and despair—bits will become lapses, and then days, and then weeks where you feel at peace—it happens.

An essential tool not only for managing a loss but also for everything that life throws your way (in particular learning to be alone) is to have a way to self-soothe, which is a fancy way of saying you must learn ways to make yourself feel better. There are many techniques, and you may need to experiment before you find ones that work for you.

The more you practice, the more your brain becomes accustomed to soothing you when you need it. Go for walks, watch movies, write in a journal, get a massage, do yoga, try a meditation retreat, watch reality TV, read books, listen to music. Each day, do one activity that helps take your mind off the stress and fear you are experiencing. Even if it only lasts ten minutes, it will help you to find clarity and manage the healing process.

Exercise: Take on a Self-Soothing Activity

- **Progressive muscle relaxation:** Go to a comfortable room, dim or turn off the lights, lie down, and close your eyes. Work systematically to go through every muscle in your body, starting with your feet, calves, and thighs, moving up to the stomach, chest, face, eyes, and head. Tighten each muscle, and then relax. Focus on the contrast between the tension and relaxation. Each time you tense the muscles, breathe in; when you release each muscle, breathe out.

- **Visual imagery:** Cultivate a visual image that brings you comfort—for example, a beach scene, a mountain scene, a lake, an image of a child or your child, an image of a pet or of a person who loves you unconditionally. Go to a quiet space, close your eyes, and bring your scene or image to mind. Work on bringing the image to life: imagine the details, the vivid color, the temperature, the way it would feel to be with the image in real life, the physical sensations. As you do this, take ten deep breaths. Each time you exhale, make the exhalation a little longer than the one before. When you recognize your thoughts have taken you away, simply refocus your attention back to the image.

- **Meditation:** Take ten minutes, sit on a pillow on the floor, and make your eyes comfortable—keep them closed or open. Take ten deep breaths. Each time you inhale, count one; exhale, count two; inhale, count three; exhale, count four; once you reach ten, start again. Notice the sensation of your chest rising and falling. Scan your body for physical sensations and points of tension, and make a mental note of what you are experiencing on a physical level (chest tense, heart pounding, stomach at ease). Work to recognize each time your mind wanders. Label it "thinking," and come back to counting or to being aware of your breaths. Wake up with awareness each time the mind wanders, and pull your attention back to your breathing. It is the shifting back to the present through focusing on your breath that eventually helps you to feel more at peace. The goal is not to turn off your thoughts or to stop thinking; we all know this is impossible! The goal is to recognize the thought streams the brain gets stuck in and then pull back, with awareness, to the present experience of breathing in and out. Do this for ten minutes a day. Don't punish yourself when you miss a day—just make sure to pick meditating back up when you become aware that you have not been doing it.

Problem: "I can't stop obsessing about my ex."
Cure: Obsess constructively.

Are you frantic to get him or her back? Are you devastated? Are you recounting all of the good times in your relationship and being self-critical, thinking you screwed it all up? As a client put it: "I ruined it!" and "My emotions overwhelmed him!" You may replay in your mind mistakes that you believe caused your ex to leave. Or maybe you are obsessing about whether you made a mistake by leaving your ex. Perhaps you keep thinking about how much time, money, and emotion you invested in the relationship, and now you are left with *nothing*.

Even if you're no longer seeing your ex, you may keep the relationship alive in your mind by reminding yourself of what he or she or you did wrong in the relationship, wondering how your ex may be spending his or her time, or hoping to catch a glimpse of him or her.

The frantic, vain efforts to make things right with your former partner or to better explain your perspective represent your mind's attempts to understand how it could be that you once felt so close to someone who now seems a distant and cold stranger. *This is part of the denial stage of grief.* Instead of accepting that you need to let go, you may be imagining conversations you wish to have with your ex, things you need to get across to make sure he or she "gets it." The effort that goes into rehashing in your mind or face-to-face with your ex about what they said or didn't say or how you reacted or didn't react is just prolonging the sting of the rejection. Alternatively, perhaps you are working to find another to replace your partner and desire to go on as if nothing in your life has changed; you wish to pretend that the hole in your heart is not really there.

Whether you are tirelessly obsessing or working to find another match, until you take a clear inventory of what occurred in your relationship, you are destined to repeat the same troublesome pattern in your next union.

Exercise: Consider Your Relationship History

This exercise is a way to obsess about your relationship in a constructive manner. After all, your identity, your future identity, and what you have done or thought about on a regular basis has changed. The person who shared your most private, softest part of your psyche is no longer there for you in the way you thought. The brain needs to come to terms with this new reality. Your mind must engage a massive reboot.

Without this step of taking a cold, hard look at the reality of your relationship (not an overly positive or negative perspective), you will remain stuck in obsessive thinking about your partner.

There is always a backstory to a relationship ending, where both parties have some responsibility in what transpired. Use this exercise to look at your relationship story.

Self-Assessment: Conduct a Relationship Autopsy

- What hurt you the most at the end of the relationship?
- Looking back, were you truly happy in the relationship or were you denying and rationalizing the hardship you experienced?
- How do you think your ex experienced you?
- What will you miss most about your ex?
- What didn't you like about your ex?
- What would you think when your ex did things you didn't like?
- What would you express that you didn't like, and how would your ex respond?
- Would you usually feel better or worse after talking with your ex about your upset?
- What would you express when your ex did things you liked? How would your ex respond?
- What did you like about being in this romantic relationship?
- What are some of your most special memories with your ex?
- What are your worst memories with your ex?
- What instances are you still holding on to that keep you angry and resentful?
- What did others tell you they liked about your ex?
- What did others suggest they didn't like about your ex?
  - Did you share their point of view?
  - Do you now?
- What were the red flags in the relationship?
  - Did you talk to your ex about your concerns or ignore these red flags?
- What stopped you from taking the red flags, your instincts, or the advice of trusted others more seriously?
  - Were you afraid to be alone? Did your ex fill a self-esteem void within you?
- What were common themes in your fights and arguments?
- What role did you play in your conflicts with your ex? Were you a nagging, angry victim, or were you an avoidant, everything-is-fine type?

Other possible roles include always wanting more, never being satisfied or tying to get away and withdraw from your ex.

- How did you feel during a fight? After?
- Did you and your ex successfully make each other feel better after a fight, or did things go unresolved for prolonged periods of time?
- Write down the top five things you would like to say to your ex.
- What are you grateful for that came as a result of knowing your ex or being in a relationship with this person?
- What do you regret about your own role in the relationship?
- If you had the relationship to do all over again, what one thing would you do differently that has nothing to do with your ex but is about you?
- What is the meanest thing you wish you could express to your ex about how they are making you feel?
- What is the kindest thing you could say to your ex?
- What hurt you the most?
- How do you think you hurt your ex the most?
- How do you think you let your ex take advantage of you?
- How did you take advantage of your ex?
- If you had a magic wand, what could your ex say to you that would make you feel better about yourself or about the loss of the relationship? Can you say this to yourself now and mean it?

Consider your responses. Make your own sort of closure by answering your questions for yourself. Now, write down in your notebook the story of your relationship: what started it, what happened during it, how its ending came to be. As you write, be sure to consider your ex's feelings and yours, your ex's character flaws and yours. Be balanced and realistic, not overly sympathetic to your ex, and not all consumed by your own perspective.

STEP 3

Take Your Emotions Seriously

Many struggle with ending difficult relationships because they can't bear to be alone. If you have a strong fear of being alone, then you may not have the tools necessary to understand and cope with your emotional world. As a result, you may use your romantic relationships as a crutch, believing you are unable to manage emotionally by yourself. Once a romantic relationship ends, you may work to avoid the pain by way of a sudden flight into health, utilizing a determined "I am fine!" approach. Or maybe you dive into a sea of denial, sinking in destructive behaviors to help forget—drugs, alcohol, food, impulsive sexual experiences, desperate efforts to reengage the ex, frenetic activity, or utter isolation are examples.

Although it may seem hard in the moment, it's far easier to begin accepting your emotions as they are. This acceptance is ultimately liberating because when it happens, your emotions will no longer govern, and you can begin creating a happy life.

Problem: "I don't want to be a drama queen."
Cure: Take your emotions seriously.

Too often I see women, although it can also be true for men, who come to therapy believing they are overly "dramatic." They tend to rely on an emotional coping strategy of pushing away much of what they are observing—along with the corollary feelings that ensue. At some point, a straw breaks the camel's back. This habitual mode collapses, and containing the uncontainable is no longer possible. Because emotional upsets have been pushed away and suppressed for so long, the emotion generated and expressed is often disproportionate to the circumstances. The outburst becomes uncontrollable, and the person involved is left ashamed at her overreaction.

The drama queen cycle tends to repeat—the woman vows to keep herself in check, pushes away her negative experiences, avoids difficult emotions, and hopes that this type of emotional flare-up will never occur again, all of which contributes to her having trouble connecting with others in a real, emotionally intimate way.

Girls and women are more than two times as likely to experience symptoms of depression than boys and men. This research[1] finding has been extensively studied and culturally cross validated. Women begin to have higher rates of depression in early adolescence, around age thirteen, and this trend continues into adulthood. Research demonstrates an important variable in girls becoming depressed, one that may explain why they are more vulnerable than boys. A study, published in the *Journal of Adolescence*[2], points to the role emotional awareness plays in female depression. Girls with low "emotional clarity"—knowing what one feels, being aware of one's emotions—have an increased risk of depression compared to their peers. The study demonstrates that emotional vulnerabilities are a precise risk factor for girls and may be responsible for their higher rate of depression compared to boys.

The inability to accurately label and describe emotions has also been linked with interpersonal issues in adulthood. Adults who have difficulty with emotional attunement share their emotions less, especially when managing difficult life events. Women who can't describe their emotions have less intimacy in romantic relationships and are vulnerable to patterns of one-sided loving.

Take the case of Suzanne. Suzanne dated men who were thrilling and exciting. That's what she liked about Marc. He was always making her laugh and sweeping her off her feet with romantic gestures. After a few months of dating, he started to become less consistent and attentive in his efforts toward her—he wouldn't call when

1   Weissman, M., Bland, R.C., Canino, G.J., Faravelli, C., Greenwald, S., Hwu, H.G., Joyce, P.R., & Yeh, E.K. (1996). Cross-national epidemiology of major depression and bipolar disorder. *Journal of the American Medical Association, 276*, 293-299.

2   Hamilton, J.L., Hamlat, E.J., Stange, J.P., Abramson, L.Y. & Alloy, L.B. (2014). Pubertal timing and vulnerabilities to depression in early adolescence: Differential pathways to depressive symptoms by sex. *Journal of Adolescence, 37*.

he said he would or would back out of plans at the last minute. When these disappointments occurred, Suzanne told herself, "Don't be high maintenance and needy; he works a lot and can't help it." Over time, she was so afraid of showing Marc any of her real emotions that she became robotic in his presence and wasn't her authentic self. When she found text messages on his phone revealing that he was engaging another woman, the pent-up emotion erupted. Suzanne lost it on Marc. She became so angry she threw a vase at him, screamed, cried, and compounded the rupture by stalking him and his new woman.

Knowing oneself emotionally does *not* mean you are overly emotional. In fact, people who describe themselves as more emotionally complicated—in the sense of having a wider range of emotional experiences and showing more awareness of their feelings—actually demonstrate healthier interpersonal adjustment and greater self-control. They are less likely to be blindsided by the actions or feelings of others and less likely to act out impulsively because they know what's going on and have been paying attention all along.

Problem: "I get blindsided by the actions and feelings of others."
Cure: Recognize you are missing data.

The avoidance of negative emotion does not work and, in fact, causes negative emotions to get stronger and more destructive. If you continually tune out your feelings and/or the feelings of others, you miss valuable data about yourself and others. After all, emotions are how the self communicates its experience of the world. If we felt nothing or were always neutral, then life would hardly matter. Feelings foster an understanding of reality; they put what is important in high definition, make goals clearer, and give life genuine meaning. Emotions provide important data about preferences and core identity. Without this data, you are missing critical information. In order to manage or regulate emotions effectively, you need to consciously reflect on what is occurring for you in the moment.

For example, Doug lived his life in action. He was a perpetually busy, physically active, professionally successful thirty-five-year-old. When something difficult happened, he just blinked away the upset or emotional pain and kept on keeping on. He never paused to reflect on what he felt or why he felt certain ways. Doug became quite depressed when his partner of five years suddenly, seemingly out of nowhere, told him their relationship was over. He felt blindsided and overwhelmed by all the painful emotions of this loss. His partner responded by telling Doug that he had been communicating his discontent for more than a year but felt Doug dismissed him. As Doug spent time understanding himself emotionally, he not only gained a better sense of why his partner left but he also started to feel better.

Effective emotional regulation enables people to better control impulses, tolerate frustration, delay gratification, and empathize with others. According to Daniel Goleman, author of *Emotional Intelligence,* the greater a person's ability to manage emotional experiences, the better his or her ability to develop healthy relationships as well as to engage successful academic and professional pursuits. As people develop a capacity for empathy and form a solid understanding for the subtleties of communication, the quality of their relationships improve.

Self-Assessment—Do You Avoid Emotion?

Take this self-assessment to find out if you allow yourself to feel your emotions. If you dismiss and minimize your in-the-moment experiences, you will lose touch with who you are as a person and be out of touch with the motives and feelings of others. The more items you endorse, the more you need to increase your emotional self-awareness.

- If you cry, it means you're weak.
- Women who talk about their feelings are drama queens.
- Even when I'm upset on the inside, I'm sure to put a smile on.
- People need to buck up and stop feeling sorry for themselves.
- When people talk about their feelings, they're just making things worse.
- Feelings should not be taken seriously.
- I am often surprised by my emotions.
- Whenever I cry, I know I am being stupid.
- Emotions are black and white; it is women that make them complicated.
- As long as I stay busy, feelings don't really bother me.
- When men cry, I want to puke.
- If I feel bad, I tell myself to get over it and grow up.
- When my friends are upset, I criticize them or tell them what to do.
- When upset, I just move on to the next thing and shrug it off.

- I feel better if I just tell myself to not think about what is upsetting me.
- I regularly tell myself that if I think positively, I will be happy.
- People who pay attention to how they feel about things are overly dramatic and not to be taken seriously.
- When my friends are upset, I remind them of how lucky they are and of all that they have in life.
- I prefer to be around men; women are too emotional.
- I pride myself on always being the logical one in the group.

Problem: "I don't know how to deal with my feelings."
Cure: Develop emotional self-awareness

Healthy emotional functioning is based upon aware attunement, or knowing what you are feeling when you are feeling it. Emotional self-awareness allows stimuli to reach your brain's cortex, where conscious reflection and problem solving occur. As you become more adept at noticing your feelings, you will find that your emotions are less likely to impinge on your relational happiness.

A popular and well-researched way to become more emotionally aware is through the skill of mindfulness. Mindfulness is a hyperalert awareness to the present moment and to what is occurring in the here and now. Emotional mindfulness means training yourself to recognize subtle cues within your body. Attunement is the opposite of pushing away or suppressing emotions and when you do it correctly, your body remains at ease. Becoming attuned requires you to pay attention to both your body and your mind.

For you to successfully manage your emotional world, it is important that you develop a belief that emotions are not fixed and uncontrollable. They actually follow a fairly predictable course. People who believe their emotions are changeable have better emotional control than people who believe emotions are uncontrollable. Emotions come and go. Your goal is to monitor them as they travel through your nervous system.

There are four components to developing healthy emotional awareness: noticing how your body is changing in reaction to emotional stimuli, finding the label that best describes what you are feeling, accepting the emotion you are experiencing, and noticing the type of attention you are giving the emotion.

~ **Notice the physical.** As a function of brain processes, emotions initiate adjustments in blood pressure, heart rate, muscle tension, and the digestive tract. There is a corresponding bodily sensation and physical urge to do something in response to most everything we feel. We have become so accustomed to our bodies' response to emotions that we often do not notice these physical manifestations. By developing physical awareness, you will increase control of your reactions. It is important to tune in, from the inside out, to changes occurring in your body.

The experience of anger, for example, usually involves feeling muscles tense and an urge to aggress. One client I worked with discovered her jaw became tight when she was angry. As she tuned into this physical sensation, she became aware of her anger long before it got out of control and became destructive. Similarly, sadness is often accompanied by heaviness in the heart and a lethargic feeling. Anxiety and fear may involve an increase in heart rate or tension in the gut, while pleasure often involves feeling a lack of muscle tension and a restful sensation.

~ **Identify what you are feeling.** The next essential component for healthy emotional attunement is your ability to choose the label that best describes what you are feeling. Many are able to do this easily, but for those who suppress their emotions, differentiating their feelings does not come without effort. Noticing sensations in your body will help you to distinguish and separate your feelings. This will let you more distinctly recognize when you are angry, sad, anxious, or happy, as well as the finer nuances between feelings. It can be helpful when stuck to ask: "What is my body trying to communicate to me about how I feel in this situation? What area of my body is the most noticeable to me at this moment, and what is it signaling?"

If you are jittery or keyed up, you are probably worried and anxious. If your muscles are relaxed and free of tension, you may feel pleasure. Examine how you feel physically in different situations and then ask yourself if this is signaling fear, sadness, hurt, or anger? As you find the label that most aptly applies to what you are feeling, you will know because identifying it should bring some relief.

This exercise takes practice because emotion can be a moving target. You may first notice your heart is beating fast and you feel anxious; as soon as you label this, you may begin to notice you feel angry toward someone and then, emerging from beneath the anger, you may find hurt. Continuing to label each emotion as it comes up will help you understand much more precisely what you are experiencing, and that will enable you to cope more effectively.

The experience of anger often reflects feeling that the world is against you. People who chronically struggle with anger have both a lack of internal emotional knowledge about themselves and a lack of awareness for how their own anger plays a role in the ways in which others treat them. The quicker you recognize it is anger you are feeling, the more likely you will effectively manage the situation.

Women, in particular, tend to turn away from anger as soon as it appears. They tell themselves that it is "bad" to feel anger. When anger is not consciously attended to and labeled, the risk of acting out in ways that are hurtful to others increases dramatically. A person may turn the anger against themselves, which opens a door that often leads to depression. Anger is adaptive; it's evolution's way of motivating us to protect ourselves through boundary setting and self-assertion. Acknowledging anger allows a person to handle it appropriately, with his or her own best interest in mind.

The typical, prominent emotion experienced when a relationship ends is sadness. If you are unable to acknowledge that you are sad because of this loss, you may react inappropriately. You may decide to pursue plastic surgery, become obsessively critical of your weight and, for good measure, relentlessly beat yourself up for all that you believe you did wrong in the relationship.

If you are sad due to the loss of a relationship, it is important to label this feeling. Without an accurate label, you may find that, instead of identifying the loss as the problem, *you come to see yourself as the problem*. Although it is quite painful, once you allow yourself to feel the loss and sadness for what it is, you will be much better prepared for your next relationship.

A client who learned to recognize that she felt loss put it to me this way: "When out of nowhere he stopped talking to me, I felt wounded, as if he had broken my leg and now I can't walk and he doesn't care in the least. But despite all of that, I miss him...then I think about how hard it would be to be myself with someone who could treat me so horribly, and I know that we would never be a good match."

If you teach yourself to be conscious of what you are really feeling, it will help you pick a new kind of partner in the future.

~ **Accept what you are feeling.** Once you have a label that aptly describes your physical experience, accept that feeling. You are not trying to replay the facts of the situation or to justify or even to talk yourself out of what you are feeling. You have the feeling, and you have labeled it. It is real. Denying it would mean you are unable to know yourself on an authentic level. Even if you judge yourself harshly and push the feelings away, they will probably come out indirectly. When you indirectly express feelings that you do not fully understand, others may see you as acting dramatically and inappropriately.

The process of accepting your emotions is not a time to conjure empathy for the other person in the situation. Just stick with what *you* are feeling. Tell yourself that it is perfectly okay to experience whatever you are feeling. Alternatively, if you say to yourself, "I don't want this. I shouldn't feel this," or "He had a busy week; I should be more sensitive to his needs," then you are invalidating yourself.

For example, if you felt a hunger pain, would you tell yourself, "I am not hungry; I have no reason to feel hungry. I must be a pig."? I hope not. Emotions work in the same way. It is important to believe what your body and mind are telling you and to remember that your experience of your life is valid. If you say, "Of course I am sad. I miss my girlfriend, and I like spending time with her," you are validating yourself. If you are angry, validate this—you can love someone and simultaneously be angry with him or her. Acknowledging anger in your own mind will not destroy a relationship.

The emotional workings of the brain are largely unconscious and automatic. We only know our emotions as a reality when we become conscious of a brain process that is already occurring. By attending to your physical sensations and labeling your emotions, you are moving emotional data from the amygdala to the brain's neocortex, which allows for more conscious reflection and problem solving about the emotional event. Once you are aware of what you are feeling, you can begin to look at your options for managing the feeling.

~ **Give kind attention to what you are feeling.** It is of utmost importance to notice the type of attention you are giving to what you are feeling. Consider if you are self-critical and, if you are, develop open-minded labels for what you are feeling and a kind, internal tone. Notice when you are using disapproving terms to describe your experience: "It is bad to feel this…I am weak for feeling sad. Why do I always feel sorry for myself?" Statements such as these muddy the water and make it impossible for you to rationally assess your circumstances.

The goal is to know what you feel without losing your self-esteem in the process. Overwhelming yourself with harsh criticism prevents you from looking at specific emotions that can be identified and eventually put into perspective. As opposed to questioning what you are feeling, simply label whatever you notice—your stomach feels tense, you feel stressed, your head burns, you feel restless, you have tears in your eyes, your heart is pounding. Attunement requires back-and-forth, conscious attention to what is occurring in your body, followed up by labeling the feeling. Examine your emotions without becoming engulfed by them.

Exercise: Feelings Table

If you have difficulty knowing what you are feeling in the moment, use this chart as an aid in labeling what it is that you are *really* feeling. Doing this will help you pay attention to the important data your emotions are giving you about yourself and the people in your life.

Emotions	Physical/ Bodily sensations	Labels to describe your experience	Action urges	Evolutionary significance
Love	Calm body, relaxed, muscles, sense of internal peace and well-being	Sense of comfort, safety, comfort with another, passion, sexual longing	Desire to be with the person, to bond with the other, to make sure the other is okay	Love bonds couples, children, families, and tribes together. It is the glue that connects people

Emotions	Physical/ Bodily sensations	Labels to describe your experience	Action urges	Evolutionary significance
Pleasure	Accompanied by the brain releasing "feel-good hormones" so you may feel increased energy, lack of physical pain. Body is excited	Delight, joy, vivaciousness, contentment, mastery, feeling lost in the moment, not thinking about the future or the past	Urge to smile, laugh, talk more with others, and reveal more about yourself	Pleasure is tonic for negative emotions and motivates us to do certain things so that we may experience more pleasure
Anger	Body feels tense, jaw clenches, and muscles tighten. There is increased body temperature and a feeling of pressure behind the eyes	Feeling unfairly treated or disrespected by others or the world as a whole, outrage, rage; feeling the self is not valued	Urge to aggress or harm another, urge to yell at someone or throw something	Anger cues the body to self-protect through physical force, self-assertion, or boundary setting
Sadness	The body wants to remain still; you feel lethargic and have a lack of energy; it may be hard to get your body to move	Loss, grief, hopelessness, rejection; feeling defeated or unwanted by others, feeling bad about the self	Urge to cry or to sit still or in one place, lack of motivation, urge to ruminate about what you did to cause the loss	Sadness is protective in that it allows the self to sit in place while grief and problem solving can take place

Emotions	Physical/ Bodily sensations	Labels to describe your experience	Action urges	Evolutionary significance
Anxiety	Brain triggers the stress hormones that cause muscle tension, restlessness, increased heartbeat, sweating, shortness of breath, stomachache	Being worried or fearful, feeling threatened by something in the environment or within a relationship (fear of losing a relationship), being in high-alert, vigilant, survival mode	Urge to be vigilant, replay events in one's mind, predict future events and desire to take control of the threat. Urge to flee or to busy the self	Anxiety triggers adrenaline so that the body goes into high alert. You become primed for action and protection
Guilt	The body feels sick, the stomach hurts, the muscles hurt. It feels as if you can't be physically at ease	Feeling like a "bad" person, feeling destructive, feeling you should be punished	Urge to make amends and to be a "better" person, urge to berate the self	Guilt keeps people in accordance with societal laws and norms designed for protecting people
Shame	Burning sensation on the face, cheeks flushing, and stomach sinking	Embarrassment, humiliation, exposure as a fraud. Fearing that a flaw will be revealed to another or to the public	Urge to flee or leave the situation, urge to become invisible and hide the self from others	Shame signifies social status in a group, keeps people in accordance with group expectations

Emotional Balance

The goal is emotional balance. Emotional balance is a blending of *thinking* and *feeling*. It means you are neither flooded by emotion nor are you flooded by rational thought. Take, for example, the death of a loved one. If you only *think* about this event, you might find yourself rationalizing the loss: the person was old, led a good life, or now is free of pain. If you continue to only *think* about the death, you will not grieve or feel sadness; this often results in feeling a lack of meaning and a sense of detachment from life. On the other hand, if all you do is *feel*, you may find that you become overwhelmed by your emotions or even depressed as a result. If you allow yourself to go in and out of both thinking and feeling, you will achieve a sense of acceptance and new meaning in life due to the event.

Merging emotion with intellect allows for new insights to develop, greater intimacy within yourself, and greater intimacy with others.

No emotion is off limits. Allow the feelings to be present without overwhelming you. Your feelings are a compass, a guide, but they are not your identity. Say things like, "I notice I am feeling ——," or "A feeling of —— is overcoming me," or "My mind is telling me that ——." This kind of language will help you gain some separation from the feeling so you can remember you are not your emotions.

Look for what's missing; look for the feeling that might be hiding. You may feel sad, but perhaps under this are anger and loneliness. Keep pulling back the layers to get to the root feeling. Suppressing the emotion and judging the emotion will only make it worse.

Exercise: Use an Emotional Spreadsheet

It is important that you begin to link your feelings with the physical sensations in your body. Be willing and open to your experience of what is going on. Instead of feeling fear or making self-criticisms, invite the emotions into the open so that you can process and eventually let them go. Recognize the energy avoidance requires and the internal tension it creates. Visualize your emotions, spread them upon a blanket, and label them.

You cannot heal what you do not let yourself know you are feeling. Denying or pushing away your emotions only makes them come back stronger to cause more destruction. In addition, the mental work involved in suppressing negative emotions and pushing away upset numbs out everything—even joy and pleasure.

Whatever comes up, you can deal with it and make room for each emotion with warm acceptance, like taking care of a child or loved one who is emotionally upset.

Force yourself to consciously reflect on what you are feeling and what you may be burying. Once a day, sit down and spend ten to fifteen minutes alone, attending to your emotional world. Notice what you are feeling. Sit back and allow it to be present while labeling the following.

- What is the emotion you are feeling?
- What are the physical sensations that accompany the emotion?
- What are the thoughts associated with the emotion?
- What judgments are you making about your emotion?
- What memories are associated with how you are feeling in this moment?
- What self-soothing action can you do (take a walk or a bike ride, do yoga, call a friend, get a massage, keep a journal, go somewhere)?
- What self-soothing thought can you think about that will bring you comfort? Examples could include: "This feeling can be here as long as it needs to be," or "I am going to be okay," or "Feelings are like the weather—they change," or "This feeling will pass."

Start reflecting on your emotions in the manner described above. Once an emotion passes, another will come along. Do the exercise again for that new emotion. Eventually, engaging even your most intense emotions in this way will become a constructive habit.

This is the path to liberation from the tyranny of negative feelings. You no longer have to live as a hostage to emotional pain because you know it will pass and you know that tuning into your emotion will help it to pass. After becoming attuned with her emotional world, Sydney put it to me this way: "I have good days and bad days. I know the pain will come and go, and sometimes it feels deep, like a cavernous void, but now I know I can bear it and it won't kill me. This makes me feel strong. Now I no longer live in fear of what I might feel, because I know what I feel and I know I can handle it."

STEP 4

Create a Life without Your Partner

Now that you have a road map for how to start managing your feelings, it's time you turn to the work of considering what life could look like without your partner. I know, I know, it may seem impossible to imagine, or you don't want to imagine, or you don't believe you can imagine…a life without your ex.

As you grieve what you thought you had and the potential future you imagined, you must also start imagining a new future where you are contented.

I'm amazed at how often a breakup or divorce becomes just the spark a person needs to start new endeavors and new jobs, develop new friendships, or start working on long-delayed dreams or goals. Losing your partner does not have to be the end of you. The sooner you begin to figure out how you want to spend your time and put this plan into action, the sooner you will start to feel positive about your future again.

Doing new things and connecting with people, without your ex dominating these activities, will help you to reconnect with life and a belief that things will get better.

Problem: "The only future I can think about is how to gain closure and/or regain my dignity."
Cure: Make your own closure.

People often tell themselves that they are staying in contact or engaging an ex because of a desire for "closure." Closure has become a popular word to describe this need, but what does it really mean? Many share the illusion (promoted by our culture's over glorification of the word "closure") that an ex will say just what they need him or her to say so they can realign their self-esteem, stand tall with dignity, and walk away unscathed. Others are looking for redemption or data to clear the fog of hurt and confusion.

People who are experiencing the ending of relationships often become so consumed by whatever they believe they invested and lost in the union—time, children, emotional resources, financial sacrifices, reputation—that they can't tolerate the anguish and so go back into the boxing ring for yet another round of wishful "closure." Hoping they will hear that special nugget of intel that explains everything, they take a break from what feels like unbearable despair by trying to better explain themselves to their exes, working to get their exes to see the light, or asking their exes more questions.

If you are falling into this pattern, then you are replaying upsetting events in your mind, imagining future conversations that likely will never materialize, all the while feeling confusion, anxiety, and hurt. Stop doing this. Hear me on this: *There is no such thing as closure delivered by an ex.* Each time you search for this chimera, you are disempowering yourself and expecting more of an ex than he or she can deliver.

Instead of this endless mental pinball game, start the process of forming your own closure. Find meaning in the loss. For example, you were meant to be your child's mother/father. You were meant to know what loss feels like now, so you will appreciate what you have later, or having this hurt now may help you to pick the right mate later. Whatever it is, find a reason why this relationship ending may have a silver lining. I'm not suggesting you deny the pain you are experiencing, but it's sometimes through pain that we recalibrate and actualize deeper desires. Good things can come from sadness and hurt.

Exercise: Stop Contact

In order to form your own closure and eventually create a life without your former partner, you need adequate mental space. If you are constantly thinking about your ex, trying to see him or her, and accepting contact or initiating contact, you do not have the space needed to begin imagining and eventually creating a life without your ex. I have worked with many people during this phase who adamantly feel they can stay in contact with their exes and simultaneously get over them. For most (if not all), this is a losing battle and only delays the work that must be done to heal.

Each time you connect with your ex, you aggravate the wound and break the scab. Some do this over and over again so that the scab is never intact long enough for it to heal. I even hear of married couples living separately for years but not actually deciding to divorce. Both living in limbo, one foot in the marriage and one foot in a single adult life—you have to pick one. Ambivalence begets neurosis.

Generally speaking, a desire to stay friends or keep in contact are denial strategies to avoid feeling the pain of letting go. If you are the one ending it, you can't have your cake and eat it too—stop contacting your ex. If you are the one left, recognize the pain you are putting yourself through by continuing to allow yourself to be around what you can't have.

Special note about divorce: If children are involved, you will have to speak to co-parent your children. Keep communication professional and minimal so you can start healing.

Self-Assessment: What Is Triggering Your Urge to Make Contact?
Each time you have the urge to make contact, answer these questions and write the answers down in your notebook.

- What were you doing before the desire to make contact started? Notice if certain activities or people trigger your contact urge.
- What were you thinking about before you wanted to make contact (examples include self-critical thoughts, memory of your ex, fear of being alone, fear your ex has forgotten you, fear your ex is with another lover)?
- How were you feeling—sad, angry, worried, lonely, peaceful? Can you sit with this feeling or distract yourself? If you allow it to, the feeling will pass without you making contact.
- How are you hoping contact with your ex will go and make you feel?
- In reality, how does contact usually go?
- What is underlying your desire to contact your ex? What's in it for you ideally?

- In reality, how do you usually feel after contact—do you typically get what you want? If so, does it wear off, leaving you with another desire to make contact?
- What do you want to say to your ex?
- What would you like to hear your ex say to you?
- How would this change your situation? Are you giving a magical power to this information? Do you recognize that no matter what your ex says, you still have to move on?

Now, reread what you have written. Try to see the futility in putting yourself through this again and again—it's like beating your head against the wall, hoping for another result.

Take a major step back, at least for a while, from your ex. It doesn't mean you will never speak again. Distract yourself with other pursuits, activities, and people. Remind yourself that contacting or reengaging your ex only postpones the inevitable work you have to do to be free of this turmoil. Ultimately, your ex doesn't have the power to fix you and make you whole again—only you do.

Exercise: Recognize When You Are Obsessing

Once contact decreases, you may find you are interacting less with your ex face-to-face but in your mind, your ex remains a constant presence. Are you replaying past scenes from your relationship—conversations, events, and images—in your mind's eye, like a movie? Alternatively, are you thinking about the new person your ex is with and how attractive he or she is compared to you? Are you imagining conversations you want to have with your ex to get him or her to want you? Obsessing or ruminating—that is, thinking of all of the possible explanations of what went wrong in your relationship—is a particularly agonizing part of the acceptance process. The thoughts can be so bombarding that it's hard to focus on your work, your children, your friendships, your family, your classes…your life.

Working with clients who are struggling to come to terms with the ending of a relationship, I have found that the constant obsessing is sometimes the most difficult hurdle to overcome, and it keeps people keyed up, anxious, and ill at ease.

Each time you obsess, try to do the three things listed below—"ABC" for short.

Awareness—The quicker you notice you are in the obsession spiral, the sooner you will get out. Develop awareness for when you are overthinking, ruminating, or obsessing about that which you can't control. Notice when you are in your head, spinning your wheels while getting nowhere and not interacting with the world around you. Tune into the signals that you are overthinking: body feeling tense, head feeling full, repetitive images or dialogue, having no sense of what's going on around you—anxious energy. Label it "obsessing."

Balance—Emotional health is in large part about balance. If you are overly internal (that is, *overthinking* events in your mind) you need to get more externally focused. Once you become aware that you are obsessing, gently remind yourself that it is natural for your brain to seek answers but that overthinking is not going to change the fact that the end has come. Balance this internal focus by doing something interactive—engaging in sports or hobbies, reading a book, doing yoga, calling a friend—get out of your head and into your life.

Control—While doing something interactive, control where your thoughts go. Over and over again, bring yourself back to the present moment. At first, this may be quite difficult. You may have to do this multiple times a day. Keep doing it; each time you bring yourself out of your head and back into your present activity, interaction, or experience, you are building self-control. You are letting your brain know that you are in charge of where it goes. You have the ability to intercept the rumination process. The more you control your thoughts, the less you will fall into the obsessive spiral.

Problem: "I can't imagine a future without my ex."
Cure: Start trying.

So often, people stay in unhealthy unions or refuse to accept the end (through obsessively thinking about the relationship, talking about it, and/or working for "closure") because they can't allow themselves to conceive of a life without their romantic partners. Fearing they can't go on without their love interests, they work to fix it or to get to the root of the problems, all to no avail. For others, they can't bring themselves to end consistently frustrating, emotionally tumultuous marriages or long-term relationships. When asked what keeps them in something so disappointing, many report they simply can't imagine life alone. And the thought of being alone brings such panic that they quickly return to the work of sustaining the unsustainable.

Stop living in fear of having no life without your significant other. All of what you thought was going to happen in your future connected to this person is no longer going to happen. You now need to let your imagination run wild with possibilities for your new future. Make space to begin imagining what life could be like, good and bad, without the other.

Exercise: Imagine a New Future

Sit somewhere calm and comfortable, and bring your notebook and this workbook along with you. Reflect on the following questions, writing down whatever comes to mind even if it doesn't make sense. The purpose of this exercise is not to be an elegant writer or to get your punctuation right; simply focus on expressing whatever comes into your head.

- What type of partner did you think you had in your ex? What kind of person did you want to be with your ex? Examples include: loving, patient, tender, fun, active, intimate, respectful, kind, generous.

- What was your ex actually like in reality? What were you actually like with your ex?

- How do your responses to questions one and two differ? Many idealize new relationships, only to be let down by the reality. Did you idealize your ex or make him or her out to be more than he or she was? Alternatively, were you your best self with your ex?

- What characteristics do you need from a partner that may have been missing in your ex and that will help you to be your best self?

- Can you imagine a different type of person you could be attracted to and how this could bring you more of what you want? What internal characteristics would this person have that would bring you closer to being your best you?

- Do you feel sick to your stomach or defeated by the idea of starting a new relationship, and does this make you cling to your old one? Remember, you do not need to start a new relationship *yet*. All you need to do at this point is to remind yourself: *when you're ready, you can and will find love again*. If you keep working on yourself, your next relationship will be better than your last.

Exercise: Create a New Reality

You are beginning to consider that you will have a future and that you will have new love, eventually. Until that time, you need to start creating a life that does not involve your ex. Below are three things to do immediately to start this new life. If you get these things in place and if you stick with them consistently, the routine of your life will change and your sense of loss will gradually fade.

- **Get a support system in place:** People in unhappy relationships typically hide the depths of their pain from their friends and family. They fear opening the box on their relationship troubles will bring embarrassment or judgment, or they don't want to burden their friends/family, or they believe their support system will no longer accept their partners into their lives. By the time a breakup or divorce occurs, the person often feels completely isolated and unknown. Build up your courage and force yourself to start telling people your story. Ideally, choose a mix of trusted family and friends (and form new friends)—tell them what you have been dealing with that led up to your breakup/divorce. Explain the backstory so people get it and get you. If you just say, "We're done," people won't connect with your pain. Let yourself be vulnerable, as this eventually will help you to feel less alone and more connected.

Talking about your feelings and your relationship issues with others will bring you clarity about what happened, decrease the shame you feel, and ultimately help you to see that there is still life out there. Strive to be open.

Open yourself up to new types of people. New people bring new perspectives, and it means you won't overburden just one person in your life. Consider joining a support group with others who are experiencing hardships and are trying to get better. Recognize that it takes an enormous amount of energy to constantly put on a brave face and pretend you are okay when you are hurting. Let down the façade so that you can use this energy to heal. This is an opportunity to be real and authentic with people. This open approach will counteract all of the alone, alienated feelings that go along with ending relationships. As you connect with others, they will share their hardships or similar experiences, and you are no longer an isolate—you are one with others.

Make yourself be brave. Ask people to do activities with you, invite people out for dinner—take the initiative in planning. Commit to two activities each week where you are forced to interact—examples include having brunch with a friend and attending a support group, having dinner with a friend and attending book club, having coffee with a friend and taking an exercise class with another friend—stay committed even when you don't feel like going or asking someone to go—force yourself.

- **Get in touch with what motivates you:** As you grieve the loss of the one you thought you wanted and the loss of who you thought you wanted to be, you also experience the soreness and pain this relationship brought into your life. Not wanting to experience this pain again, you begin to reflect on who you are at your core and what you truly need for fulfillment. Reflect deeply on what brings you happiness and contentment—separate from your romantic relationships. Here are some questions to consider as you reflect:

What pursuit can you devote yourself to, now that you have time on your own? What gives you a sense of meaning as an individual? What's your purpose in being here, and what is the legacy you want to leave behind? What tasks are easy for you to do or that you look forward to doing? On days when you have felt satisfied at the end of the day, how have you spent your time?

If you are having difficulty connecting with something that moves you and brings you enthusiasm, try to go back to your childhood. What memory do you have of yourself as a kid when you were deeply engaged or interested in a specific activity? Can you bring any of this into your life now and eventually into your future relationships?

You may find this exercise hard. It may seem like there's nothing you are interested in. Keep reflecting and trying out things—everyone has something.

- **Make long-term goals:** Review each facet of your life—achievement, finance, health, social/family, and joy—and make specific goals for each domain.

For example, review your *accomplishments*, lack thereof, or areas for growth and development. You may want to push for something at your job, or perhaps you don't work, but you want to take on a class or new job to experience a sense of achievement.

Review your *financial situation*. Make goals for saving, or disentangling your finances from your ex, or becoming more financially empowered.

Consider your *health*, and make goals to take good care of yourself physically. Divorce and difficult relationships take a physical toll, and it's important to know where you stand medically so you can rebuild. Make an appointment for a medical physical with blood work. Take on an exercise program and/or better nutrition.

Review your *social and family life*. Make goals for developing broader connections that no longer involve your ex. Make goals for finding hobbies that you can share with new friends and/or family members.

In terms of *joy*, it's important that you start scheduling time for pleasure. At first, you may not feel up for it, but try. Enjoy a nice meal, book a massage, take yourself to a movie, share a gigglefest with a friend. Building pleasure into your life helps to buffer the hardship.

STEP 5

Work on Your Relationship—
with You

People caught in the trap of unhappy relationship patterns sometimes avoid looking at their own flaws and areas of needed growth by focusing all of their attention on sustaining the unsustainable. By focusing on their partners and continually having to work through relationship conflict and disappointment, they have few emotional resources left to deal with their own issues. As the years progress, their issues continue to go unaddressed, and they become increasingly dependent on staying in relationships with people who disappoint, subsisting on the inconsistent momentary highs. As a result, a person in this situation makes countless sacrifices in terms of his or her own personal growth. At the heart of this struggle is often an agonizing fear of being alone and a desire to avoid it at all costs.

If you are searching for someone to take you away from your fear of being alone, then you might be prone to picking partners who aren't really good for you but fill a void—or as one client put it to me: "Warm bodies. I'm so afraid of being alone I just look for a warm body to fill the space and don't think about what they are actually like as people." These "warm bodies" may help you momentarily escape being alone but in the long run, they perpetuate your fear of it.

People who can be peacefully alone and enjoy their aloneness have an advantage when it comes to love and romance. By not starting relationships already at a deficit (in desperate need for a "drug" to take them out of their feared state of aloneness), they make better decisions about those they allow into their lives.

Problem: "I can't stand to be alone."
Cure: Build a relationship with yourself.

An important fact is that we are attracted to people who treat us the same way we treat ourselves. If you can't stand to be alone with yourself, you may find that you are constantly the one initiating contact with your partners. You may find you can't count on their undivided attention and feel you always have to compete with the many demands in their lives. As you come to value you and enjoy you, you will be attracted to others who want to spend time with you in a similar way. After all, if you can't stand to be with yourself, who else will?

It's very common after a breakup to want to fill the internal void with another relationship—some are able to resist this impulse, while others find themselves giving in to it over and over. Or if they can't yet find suitable relationships, they may fill the void by hypersocializing and working hard to meet new partners. Some feel completely at a loss if they don't have or are not in the process of developing a romantic crush. This constant frenzy of meeting and greeting prevents you from confronting the one thing that will liberate a person from the cycle of always having to have a warm body present. You need to start enjoying being on your own, in your own head, in your own body, with no distractions.

You may be saying, "I have heard all of this before. 'Work on you.' But what does it really mean to be okay on your own?" There are two important components of getting along better with yourself. First, change the voice in your head to be a friend and champion of you. And second, schedule regular periods of time alone so that you may, without distraction, learn to be more comfortable with yourself.

Become Aware of the Voice in Your Head

Every person has a voice in his or her head. The voice comments on what you are observing and experiencing in the world around you. The voice critiques, judges, and tells you how to think about your experiences. As you read this sentence, pause quietly and listen for what your internal voice is saying to you. Maybe it's saying, "What's she talking about? I don't have a voice!" or "I don't want to read about this subject anymore," or maybe your voice is telling you, "I need a nap." If at first you don't think you have one, consider that may be your voice telling you that you don't have one.

Your voice likely changes in tone, intensity, and harshness, depending on what you are feeling and what's going on in your environment. Pay close attention to how your voice speaks to you. If you are going through a difficult time or generally have trouble being alone, there is a strong chance that your internal commentary is harsh, critical, and overly intense. This makes it hard to be alone with yourself, and you may use other people (or even destructive behaviors) to avoid this self-critical monologue. After all, who wants to be around a friend or family member who always says, "I told you so," or points out your flaws, areas of weaknesses, or how you overreact emotionally? Imagine a friend who, every time you hit a setback, tells you what you did to cause the problem and reminds you of all the times in the past you did the same "bad" thing?

Friends and relatives who make us feel good about ourselves and comfortable being ourselves are the ones we are typically most at ease with. You must start relating to yourself in the way a warm and kind friend or family member would.

Changing the voice in your head to be more supportive and nurturing of you will help you to be more comfortable when alone—and negative internal thoughts will recede.

The fear of being alone is real and palpable. Over the years in my psychotherapy practice, I have talked to many women and men who get to this step and confess to me that they have an overwhelming fear of being alone. One sixty-five-year-old woman filed for divorce from the same man three times and struggled to find a reason to remain in her lonely marriage. Yet she could not bring herself to follow through. I asked, "How about taking some time, on your own?" She responded she had never had a time in her life when she was on her own. She married in her early twenties and before that had a series of serious boyfriends. The thought of being on her own was paralyzing. I reminded her that she was already feeling alone even though she was married. She responded, "Yes, but I know how to be alone in a marriage. I don't know how to be alone by myself."

A woman in her early thirties was caught in a repetitive cycle of strongly wanting to break off her long-term relationship and then talking herself out of it. I asked, "How about some time on your own?" She responded that she didn't think she could handle it. I asked her if she could imagine herself in an apartment alone, hanging out with friends on the weekends, going to work and participating in activities during the weekdays—she responded that all she could see was darkness.

Typically, when people dig deeper into their fear of being alone, it's not the aloneness itself that's so scary. It is what they tell themselves (that is, what the voices in their heads are telling them) the alone state means about them. For many, it means unlovability—"No one wants me," "I'm unlovable," "I don't belong," "I will be alone forever," "I'm doomed to a life alone," "I'm permanently flawed," "I feel cast out."

Self-Assessment: Consider These Questions to Become More Aware of Your Internal Voice

- What is the tone? Is it loud and impatient, or is it warm and tolerant of what's going on with you and your immediate world?
- When you're upset, does your internal voice try to soothe you, or does it use intense/judgmental language that makes you feel worse? Examples of judgmental language: "That was bad," "You suck," "You are never going to get this right," "People hate you," "You're an inadequate mother/father."
- Generally, what are the themes running through your head? The more you pay attention, the more likely you will see similar things repeating: "I screw everything up," "I'm always behind," "I'm different and don't fit in with others." The points of repetition will give you a pretty good idea of what you need to learn to feel better about.
- Does your internal voice take away your moments of joy? When you are happy or feel at ease, does your voice intrude by telling you things you need to work on and tasks that need to be accomplished or bringing to mind anxious/worrying thoughts?
- Are there certain tasks, hobbies, or people that bring out a kinder, warmer side of you, where your internal voice seems softer, less

critical? If so, these are the kinds of things you should do more of and the types of people you should be around more often. If not, experiment with different activities and people to find those that bring out your softer side.

Exercise: How to Change the Voice in Your Head

The goal is to be on good terms with yourself, regardless of the status of your relationships or of what's occurring in your life. Showing yourself unconditional love means you don't berate yourself for your weaknesses and you don't dampen the moments of joy you would otherwise experience.

Work to make the tone of your internal voice kind, warm, and understanding—similar to how you would talk to a child who is upset about something. If you need to examine what you did wrong in a situation or take responsibility for something, bring this to your attention with warmth and empathy. Don't say, "*You suuuuck. You shouldn't have called him again. You are so needy and pathetic!*" Instead say, "You are hurting, you are lonely, and it's hard not to have that connection with him anymore. You will feel better if you stop contacting him so you can stop reinjuring yourself and start healing."

When going through the loss of a relationship, the most painful emotions are related to reminding yourself of all of the things you did wrong and reminding yourself of all the things your partner did wrong. This negative-thinking spiral can make you physically ill and derails the healing process.

Pay close attention to promoting self-talk that involves self-compassion and forgiveness. Self-compassion means showing yourself a warm understanding of your perceived inadequacies. Forgiveness means voicing a less harsh internal monologue about your ex.

So instead of pretending everything is fine or that everything is catastrophic, you simply exist with your pain while also being kind and gentle with yourself. If your internal voice is filled with anger and resentment toward your partner, then you are poisoning the healing process. As you process the end of your relationship, of course you need to take stock of what your partner was like and how he or she impacted you. Do this without harsh language. Instead of, "She's a terrible person," it becomes, "I felt unloved by her," or "We didn't have enough in common." Change your internal dialogue from the kind of person your partner may be to the impact your ex's behavior had on you and your life. Instead of using black-and-white/judgmental language, start the process of forgiveness by internally noticing what was healthy and unhealthy for you and less about what kind of character your partner has.

You Can't Avoid *You*

You can never avoid being alone completely. Not accepting this fact causes a great deal of turmoil. Some people are perpetually social, always around others, striving for validation, yet when the curtains close and no one is around, they are empty and feel they have nothing. Nothing is not "bad." Nothing is a blank canvas for you and allows you to take a break from having to be there for others, take care of others, or gain your value from others.

Feminine energy often manifests in a robust aptitude for noticing and reacting to the needs and feelings of those around them. Girls are socialized for empathy, care, and responsiveness to others. Caring and relating can become a trap when a person becomes so committed to staying close to others that she loses touch with her separate sense of self. At the extreme, self-esteem may come to depend almost entirely on relationships with others. In that case, being alone with time to fill may provoke panic and the sense of having done something terribly wrong.

People in this situation may find themselves in a revolving door state, where romantic partners enter and exit their lives quickly. Not wishing to be alone, a person may work overtime to play a role that they believe will make them acceptable. Playing a role to please someone else takes you further away from knowing and accepting your true self. And too, playing a role is emotionally draining.

Another strategy for coping with the fear of being alone is constant motion. Business can be a distraction, but the anxiety generated by an endless need to find distractions is hard to tolerate.

Working to avoid being alone is a losing battle—it might be those ten minutes driving in the car, not being able to fall asleep at night, waiting for someone to show up, wondering if someone will show up—inevitably, everyone will find themselves unaccompanied from time to time. For the perpetually overbooked, the unfamiliarity of suddenly finding themselves alone with no distractions feels unnatural and even shocking. The distress is compounded by a lack of knowledge for how to fill the space, for how to be comfortably alone.

If you can't stand to be alone with yourself, then how can you attract friendships and partners who truly value being with the real you?

Exercise: Stare Yourself Squarely in the Eye

Sit quietly and reflect for ten minutes each day without noise from the outside world. At first, you may feel uncomfortable, but simply notice/label what you are experiencing. Learn to be aware of what's going on in your body when no one is around to fill the space. Ask yourself: What are you avoiding by never being alone with yourself? What's the hardest part of being alone for you? Allow those feelings to be experienced without actively pushing them away or judging yourself—just stare yourself down. You can take it.

Even if the answers to these questions are not, at first, easy to articulate, by taking time to reflect, you remind yourself that you are a separate entity worthy of your own close attention. Repeat to become more and more comfortable with this exercise. Habituate yourself to your own aloneness, and see that nothing awful happens if you treat yourself kindly in your head. It may be like a new house—at first, it feels unfamiliar but over time, you will become more and more accustomed to the rhythms of your body and the thought streams that come up for you when you are on your own.

Exercise: Schedule Alone Time

Commit two hours a week to doing activities completely on your own that reflect what you want to be doing (not what others think you ought to do or want you to do for them). The more you commit to your scheduled alone time, the sooner it will become natural and even enjoyable. Examples include having a night alone each week to watch TV or cook a meal for yourself, or an afternoon where you ride your bike or go to a movie (remember, though—go alone). Take a class on Saturday mornings where you don't know anyone in the class or attend a concert or performance on your own. If you have children, still commit to two hours alone once a week—get a babysitter if possible.

Fill your alone time with activities that interest you. Once you enter a new relationship, you will have a framework for existing on your own, separate from your new partner. This means you have things that make you happy, even if the relationship is not ideal or even if you feel let down or disappointed by your partner. Having a life outside of your romantic relationships is an enormous safeguard to emotional hardships, helps with perspective, and takes pressure off new relationships.

Learn to appreciate your solo time, and look forward to your "Tuesday nights" alone—getting to watch a show you like, eating food you like, or reading quietly without distractions. Call your weekly alone time something in your mind so you can remind yourself of it in a positive way—one client I worked with called it her "two-hour, *all-me* time." Being alone does not mean you are rejected; it means you can do whatever you want, and you don't have to explain it, justify it, request it, or rationalize it for others in your life. Look at alone time as free time—no pressure, just peace within yourself.

Final Note

Letting go is a potent mechanism of self-help. Comfort for the tenderest heartache is the self-knowledge that, despite the loss, one has put his or her own health first. This knowledge is reparative and begins a cascade of positive change and feelings of well-being.

People who struggle with romantic relationships wonder if something is wrong with them that they can't find or sustain healthy love, and they tend to beat themselves up with the possibilities—women in particular worry about their appearance, weight, and personality, while men worry about appearing physically strong or financially powerful. There may be some things you need to tweak but likely not the things you think. Instead of berating yourself trying to figure out what you are missing, get to the work of enriching the deeper you.

Allow yourself a period of time to be single long enough to become comfortable with you, all on your own. Consider perusing the other workbooks in this series. *Building Self-Esteem* will help you appreciate yourself just as you are. Understanding your negative love patterns is explored in *Toxic Love*. Dating will come later and is worked through in *Getting Close to Others*. For now, take the pressure of having to find someone off your plate and give yourself the opportunity to form a tight relationship with you, from the inside out.

Summary of the Five Steps

Step	Action to take
#1 Accept you need to let go	You can do this. Take a hard, cold look at the dysfunction in your relationship; face the facts of what's been going on between the two of you. Do not romanticize
#2 Know how to let go	Give yourself over to the process. This will take time; you need to feel the pain to heal the pain. Tell people your breakup/divorce story, self-soothe, obsess constructively
#3 Take your emotions seriously	Begin treating your feelings as data about what's going on around you: what you like and don't like as intel. Stop avoiding and living in fear of your feelings. Actively reflect each day on how you are feeling. Use the emotional spreadsheet
#4 Create a life without your ex	Make space to begin imagining a life without your partner. To do this, you need to *stop contacting your ex* and to build awareness for how the obsessive spiral takes you away from being present in your real life. Use the "ABC" strategy
#5 Work on your relationship with you	Spend ten minutes a day experiencing yourself alone. Work to notice your internal voice and how it speaks to you. Spend two hours a week doing things you enjoy on your own

AFTERWORD

What Is the Relationship Formula?

reaking Up and Divorce is part of the Relationship Formula Workbook Series, which consists of four brief workbooks designed to help people who struggle with relationships. Whether you are married, single, divorced, newly starting your dating life, gay, or straight, this workbook series will increase your relationship preparedness so that you may better find healthy, meaningful partnerships.

As a psychologist, I see people who talk about feeling they are "emotionally flawed" and "incapable of finding healthy love" or who describe a history of dating "losers" or a series of chronically disappointing relationships. They say they have "repetitive relationship issues" and fear they will never crack the code for love and romance, telling me, "I have never had a *real* relationship," or beating themselves up with, "What is wrong with me that I can't get what seems so easy for everyone else?"

If you can't get relationships right, constantly feel as if something is wrong with you when it comes to romance, and/or find you are continually drawn to the same kinds of disappointing or dysfunctional partners, then the Relationship Formula Workbook Series offers a way to gain control. Before you pick your next romantic partner, give yourself an opportunity to be all you can be—because that process will help you find all you deserve.

People who struggle with feeling good enough to get what they want out of life or those who have a history of unfulfilling relationships typically benefit

BREAKING UP & DIVORCE

from learning new skills. These four workbooks cover managing four key areas of growth:

1. *Breaking Up & Divorce 5 Steps: How to Heal and Be Comfortable Alone*
2. *Building Self-Esteem 5 Steps: How to Feel "Good Enough" about Yourself*
3. *Toxic Love 5 Steps: How to Identify Toxic-Love Patterns* and *Find Fulfilling Attachments*
4. *Getting Close to Others 5 Steps: How to Develop Intimate Relationships and Still Be True to Yourself*

Many who struggle with relationships alternate between self-blame for not "getting it right" or inflating and romanticizing what they think others have that they can't get. The statistics on marital abuse, distress, and infidelity paint a different picture. Many marriages are based on unhealthy relationship patterns of codependency, avoidance, living entirely separate lives, and in some cases, emotional abuse. Half of marriages result in divorce, and more than half of second marriages result in divorce. Even couples who stay together for a lifetime aren't necessarily happy or healthy. The reality is relationships take work, and even people who are married or appear to have it all have not always done the necessary work.

The Relationship Formula is not about telling you whom to date; rather, it focuses on the one part of romance that you can control—yourself.

The impact relationships, in particular romantic ones, have on our lives cannot be overstated. They influence physical health, psychological well-being, professional success, lifespan, pleasure, and the emotional success of our children or future children. When you decide working on yourself is a priority, you are taking a step that will powerfully influence the trajectory of most aspects of your life. This change has the potential to ripple out to every relationship—close friendships, parents, siblings, nieces, nephews, work colleagues, and classmates, as well as children born and unborn. By building yourself up, you acquire the capacity to build others up.

Relationships have the power to heal, to connect, and to provide immeasurable warmth to buffer life's harshest realities. On the flip side, destructive relationships are also powerful and can do crushing harm. You have the ability to choose which path you take. If you decide to take this one—that is, building yourself up from the inside out—work on believing with every fiber of your being that if you persevere, life will get better.

The Relationship Formula Workbook Series is designed to be used on your own or together with a therapist. Oftentimes, working with a therapist can be tremendously effective in understanding yourself and building more positive patterns of interacting. For others, going to therapy requires more expense or time than they have. Some simply prefer to do this work on their own. However you approach the work is okay, provided persistence rules.

This program is modular, with four separate workbooks. Some may wish to go through all four. Others will prefer to tailor their approach to their specific histories and issues. It is absolutely fine to complete one workbook or to go forth and complete all four. As you read through the steps, you may come up with your own strategies or find idiosyncratic ways to combine the various tools to suit your personality or personal struggle. Keep a notebook of your work so you can review what you have written down and have learned about yourself as you grow through this program. The more you review the material, the more the tools described will become automatic.

The work may seem daunting at first, but what is far harder is a lifetime of frustrating and disappointing attempts at securing love. Just like beginning a new physical exercise program, it's difficult initially but with time, the routine becomes easier and easier. You will notice progress, begin to feel better, and have more positive interactions with others. These rewards will reinforce and, day by day, you will grow.

Made in the USA
San Bernardino, CA
14 February 2019